Who were the Romans anyway?

Written by Laura Cowan

Illustrated by Victoria Stebleva

Designed by Anna Gould

With expert advice from Dr. Shushma Malik,
Associate Professor in Classics,
University of Cambridge

Why is this guy wearing
a bear on his head?

Because he can.
Find out more inside...

In this book you might come across some words to do with
Romans that are new to you. If you want to check what
they mean, turn to the word list on pages 44-45.

Usborne Quicklinks

For links to websites where you can find out more about life in Roman
times, visit **usborne.com/Quicklinks** and type in the title of this book.

Usborne Publishing is not responsible for the content of external websites.
Children should be supervised online. Please follow the online
safety guidelines at **usborne.com/Quicklinks**.

Who WERE the Romans anyway?

Well... they were people who lived a very long time ago. They came from a place called Rome in Italy.

At first, Rome was a tiny place – probably full of sheep and farmers. But it became... a **powerful** city. It was so powerful, Romans ended up in charge of the **whole** of Italy. They made a super strong army and sent it to take over lots of other places. Then the other places became Roman, too. All the places Romans ruled made up an *empire* – so big and exciting, people still **love** talking about it today. It was called the **Roman Empire**.

How BIG was their empire?

Pretty big. Today there are **fifty** countries where the Roman Empire used to be. It stretched across **Europe**, as well as some of **North Africa** and **West Asia** – everything orange on this map is **Roman**.

Emperor Hadrian had a wall built here to keep out people from further north.

A Roman general named **Julius Caesar** conquered this bit for Rome.

This was **Roman**.

SALVE! That's how Romans say "hello". It's LATIN – the language Romans speak.

Who started it?

According to Roman legend, Rome was founded by **Romulus**. (ROME-ulus, get it?) He and his twin brother **Remus** were raised by a mother wolf, so wolves were a special animal to Romans.

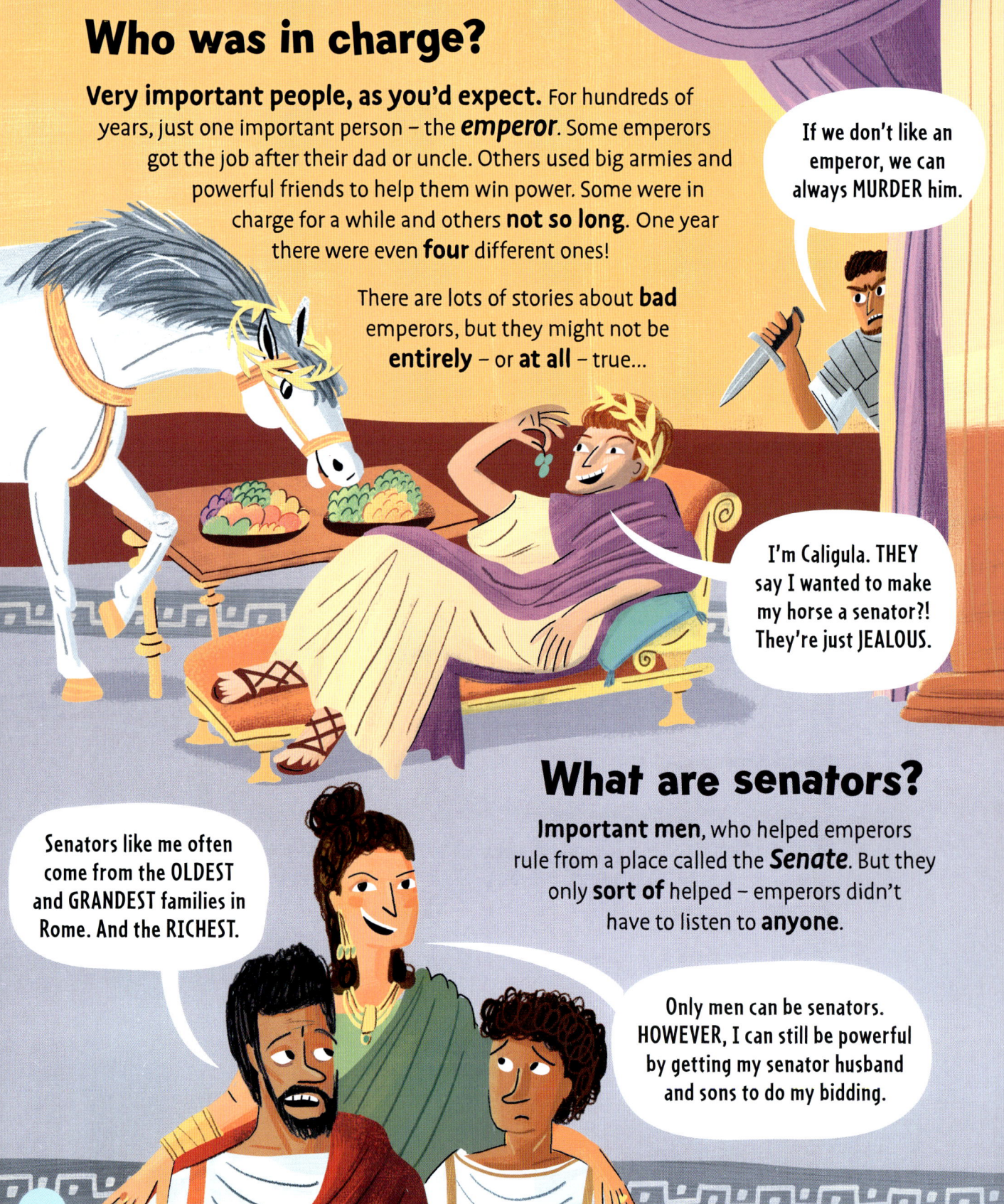

What did they look like?

What do people look like? All sorts! They came from all across the Empire – and sometimes beyond – so they all looked different. Lots of them wore similar kinds of clothes, though...

Like WHAT?

This guy is an ordinary Tomus, Dickus or Harrius.*

He's wearing a **tunic** and a pair of sandals.

Caecilius is draped in a massive semicircle of fabric called a **toga**. Some togas were so big, you could probably live inside one.

Livia here is sporting a **stola**, a kind of dress, worn over a tunic.

She's teamed it with a cloak called a **palla**.

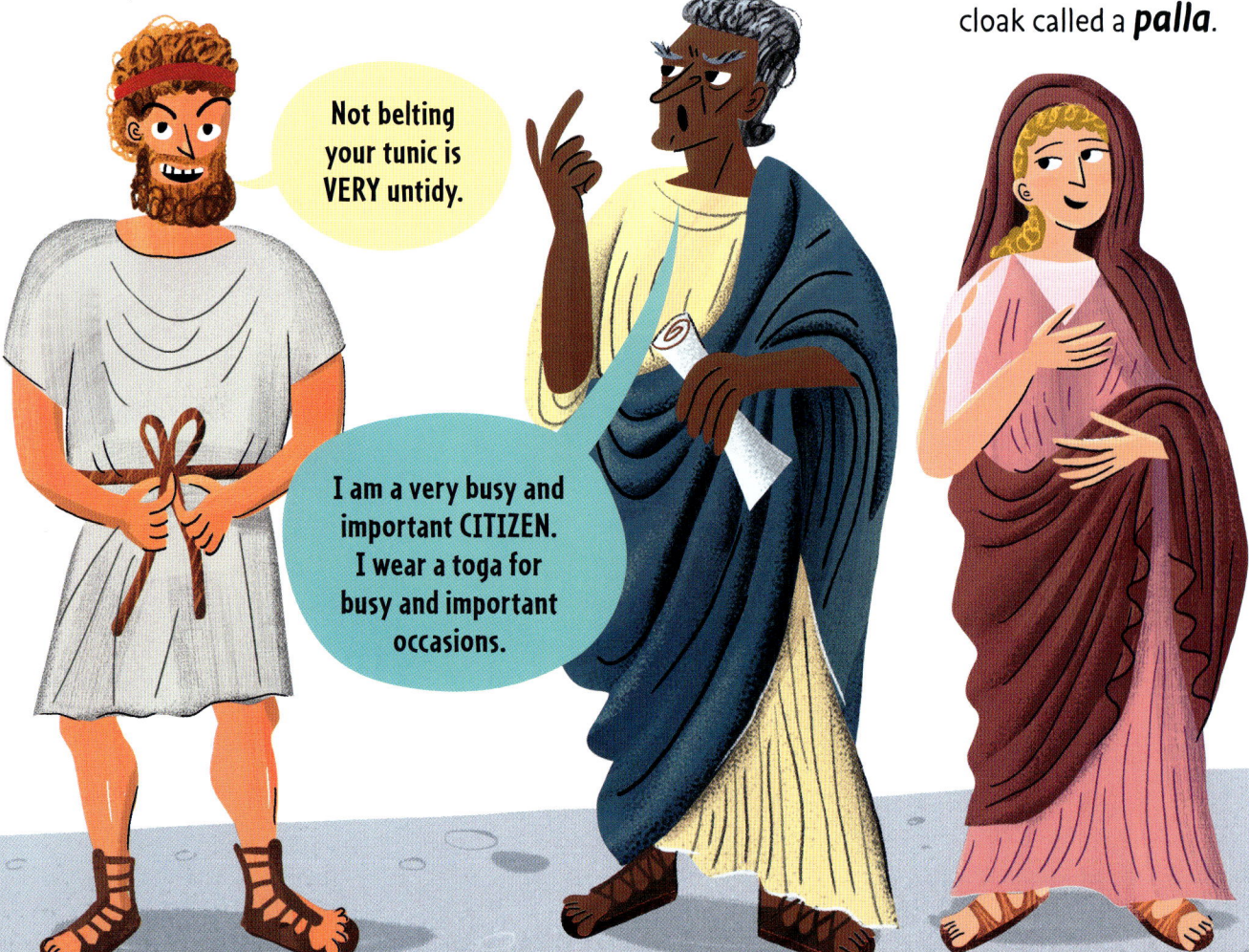

Not belting your tunic is VERY untidy.

I am a very busy and important CITIZEN. I wear a toga for busy and important occasions.

*Guess what? Roman men's names often end with -us.

How did their clothes stay on?

Roman clothes didn't zip up, but they did have pins and a kind of brooch called a **fibula** to fasten them. Romans could also cinch their waist with a nice belt.

What were their clothes made of?

Wool from sheep, linen from the flax plant, occasionally cotton, and for very wealthy Romans, silk from China. Some Romans thought silk was a bit **rude**, because it could be see-through. Oo, pardon my bottom!

Do you like my belt? It makes my eyes POP!

Oof, why do I feel so CHILLY all of a sudden?

Some clothes were so nice, they might get stolen...

How did they do their hair?

Men who could afford it went to the barber, called a **tonsor**. He styled their hair and shaved their faces or trimmed their beards. Over the years, beards went in and out of fashion.

This mirror is not that great for looking at yourself. It's just shiny polished metal!

I would like to look like the EMPEROR HIMSELF, please.

Did Romans wear BLING?

Men might dye their hair and paint their faces, too – but maybe pretend they didn't.

Yes! Wealthy Romans **loved** bling. Some Roman writers complained about their fellow Romans wearing **too much**.

Women wore necklaces, earrings, bracelets and headbands made from gold and precious stones – or ivory, from elephants' tusks. Some young women even wore **anklets**.

Men **and** women wore rings. Stylish Roman men wore lots at once. They also wore pendants.

And their faces?

Women with money had other women at home to do their hair and paint their faces. Many women (and men too) liked using skin products and perfumes.

They put some **odd** things on their faces – lead paste to make their faces white. It's very poisonous, but they didn't know that. Chalk mixed with vinegar was safer, but also **terrible** for skin.

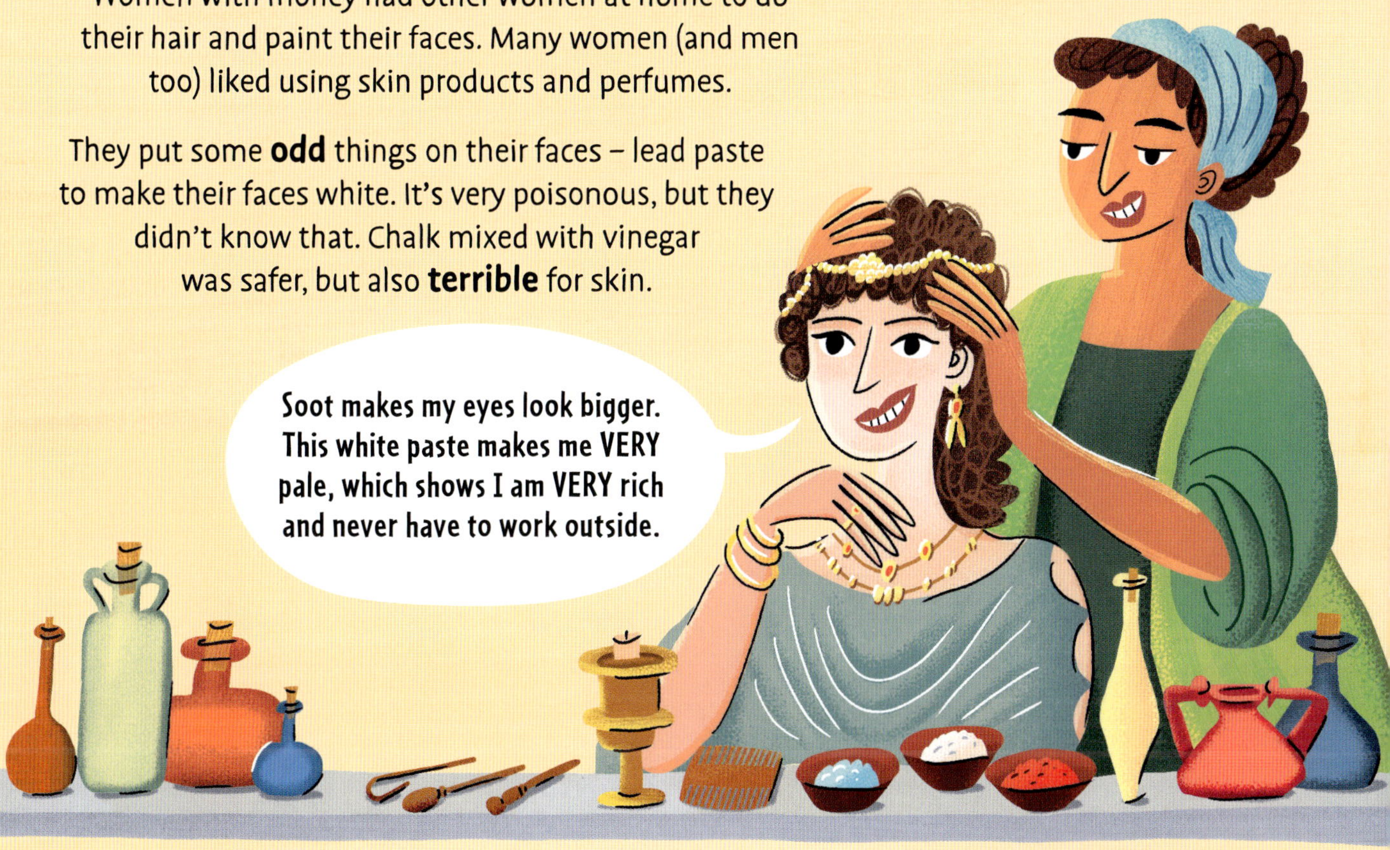

Soot makes my eyes look bigger. This white paste makes me VERY pale, which shows I am VERY rich and never have to work outside.

Rich women's hairstyles became **crazier** and **crazier** as the years wore on...

This is actually a WIG, but SHHHH...

What were their homes like?

Not that different from ours – well, unless you were the Emperor Hadrian. He had a massive palace in the countryside that was big enough to fit a whole town in.

Very big houses in the countryside were called **villas**. Some were **enormous**, but this is just an ordinary one. Still pretty big actually. Like lots of lovely villas, it's got a courtyard in the middle with a beautiful fountain. And there's underfloor heating – snug...

This villa has an orchard and a herb garden, as well as a farm.

Lots of enslaved people worked in villas – cooking, cleaning, gardening, farming and serving the family.

Where did most people live?

In cities. Nearly everyone lived in apartment buildings called *insulae*. They could be as tall as nine levels – pretty impressive without mega construction machinery!

> The top floor is the WORST! There are A LOT of stairs to climb, no running water, and if there's a fire, we're STUCK.

> The high-up levels are small and DANGEROUS, so super CHEAP!

There's a shared toilet on the street level. But you can also use a bucket and chuck it **out of the window**.

There are bigger apartments for people with more money, but many apartments are small. There's only really room to sleep.

> I own this insula and I have a luxurious CITY home too. It's called a DOMUS.

There are usually shops on the street level.

People rent the apartments from this wealthy landlord.

How did they make their houses look GOOOOOD?

Well, Romans **loved** giant paintings called *frescoes*. These weren't paintings in frames – they were painted straight onto walls.

Some frescoes show scenes from **fantastical** stories – like this guy riding some kind of magical sea horse.

First, the artist puts on all the bright paints. Then, when it's dry, he'll add the lighter, pastel ones.

Don't use too much purple – it's the most expensive. It comes from a sea snail's bottom, don't you know!

Where are the lights?

They're called windows? Just joking. Romans didn't have electricity or gas, like we do today, but they did have oil. They burned the oil in lamps to make light at night.

What were their kitchens like?

Big houses had **big ones** with lots of servants cooking different food on different fires. Apartments didn't have kitchens at all – people bought cheap ready-cooked food.

Lying down makes me SO hungry...

I can't see any beds?

Nope. Roman beds look more like couches. Rich Romans had lots of beds for all kinds of things – eating, studying and just hanging out.

Ordinary Romans probably just had one for sleeping. Enslaved people might have slept on animal skins and piles of leaves instead.

Do you like my mosaic floor? I paid lots of very clever men to make it by pressing tiny stones into wet plaster.

Well, I've got the most FANTASTIC fresco. It looks like a WINDOW but it's actually a painting.

Where's the toilet!?

At its biggest, the Roman Empire had 144 public toilets.
But, of course, important wealthy people did not want to use the bathroom with any old person. They had their own at home.

Did they have toilet paper?

No, but they did have sponges on sticks and other things. After they'd used the sponge, they gave it a little rinse in water and left it for the next person. **Mmm!**

We call this a TERSORIUM.

I'm scraping my bottom clean with pieces of broken pot called PESSOI.

My boss paid for this public toilet to be built – mainly to stop ordinary people like me doing their business in the streets.

Big jobs

Public toilets were mostly for men. They didn't have cubicles – everyone sat together to do big jobs. Little piddles went into jars or just on the street.

Where did they get all the water?

From *aqueducts*. An aqueduct is basically a really, really long pipe running downhill. It takes fresh water from a lake or spring to a city or town. Romans built **loads** of them.

Some of the water is piped to rich people's homes.

Water runs down here.

Where did it all go?

Rome had a **great** system for dealing with dirty water. Often public toilets were next to public baths, so the dirty water from the baths could wash the plops away into the sewer.

The sewer took all the dirty water out of towns and cities and into... some rivers. But sometimes the sewers flowed back up onto the streets. **Ew!**

The middle of the sewer system in Rome is called CLOACA MAXIMA – which means "greatest drain". It really is THE GREATEST.

Bleurgh – the greatest STINK!

Did Roman children go to school?

Only some of them. They were lucky if they got the chance – lots had to go to work instead! Romans who could afford it paid for tutors at home or sent their children to small schools.

What did they learn?

Reading, writing, counting and **memorizing**. Older boys also learned **Greek** and **public speaking**.

"Hello, teacher! Hello, fellow pupils!"

Children are expected to be **very** polite, like this.

The man here is a **paedagogus**. His job includes walking a child to school and back, and helping with homework.

"I'm trying to learn this GIANT poem and then I have to recite it to the teacher. YAWN."

This is a small school called a *ludus*, for children under eleven. It's behind a curtain at the back of a shop.

Scratch scratch

1, 2, 5, OOPS.

The teacher is an enslaved person from Greece. Romans thought Greek education was **the best**.

Where is your money for today's classes, Flavius?

When's lunch!?

GURGLE

These children ate breakfast before the sun came up. So they're quite hungry now.

Rumble

Pass me my new tablet, Felix!

Felix carried all this boy's things to school, and now he has to wait here. Felix is not getting paid for this, because he's an enslaved person, too.

What did they write on?

Tablets. But you couldn't do fun things on them, like play games. These ones were wooden and filled with hard wax. (From **bees**, not inside your **ears**.)

To write on the wax tablet, they scratched into it with a stick called a **stylus**.

To rub out a mistake, they used the flat end of the stylus.

Holding a flame under the tablet melted the wax and erased **everything**, so they could start again.

Holding a flame too near would set fire to the tablet. Oops!

"I have five writing tablets, your stylus and your scroll case in the bag."

Were Roman schools hard work?

Oh yes. School was from sunrise to sunset, with only a short break for lunch (although some **lucky** children went home for lunch and some didn't go back). Thankfully, Romans had lots of public holidays.

What happened if Roman children MISBEHAVED?

Nothing good. Some teachers were **very** strict. Students were expected to pay attention and be very polite. Really naughty children might be **beaten** or **whipped**.

Where are all the girls!?

You might spot one or two. Not many girls went to school. Girls from rich families often learned reading and writing at home – maybe playing music and singing, too.

Girls from less wealthy families learned how to look after a home and trained in their family business. Mostly, Romans weren't **super** interested in girls learning school things, but some girls were taught them anyway.

...and he said "you didn't, you're lying," and I said "look, it's on my tablet, stupid!"

Where are all the books?

Not invented yet! Romans had rolled-up **scrolls** made of animal skin or **papyrus** – paper made from reeds. Copies were made by enslaved people. They had to write out each scroll by hand, which took **ages**. Later, Romans **did** have books, made of papyrus pages stitched together. This kind of book was called a **codex**.

There might only have been a few scrolls at a ludus. They wouldn't have had fun stories in them either – they were probably used for learning Latin.

What were all the other children doing!?

Working. Some children worked with their parents in their workshops or farms. These children probably didn't learn to read and write **at all**.

PLEASE just WALK, COW!

Did Romans go shopping?

They sure did! And there were all kinds of places to go, depending on what they needed.

Where did they buy food?

From markets! Sometimes people went to a big indoor food market called a *macellum*.

There are pictures of the food on the walls, to show what's for sale.

Meat!

Fresh fish! Straight from Mare Nostrum!

I'd like some pork loins, some pork sausages, also ham? We do love pork, don't we, Hector?

Marble counters keep everything cool.

Did they have shopping malls?

Not exactly. In any Roman town or city, the main marketplace was a place called the *forum*. A bit like a mall, it wasn't just for shopping – it was for meeting friends, **serious discussions**, big debates and hanging out.

The Emperor Trajan built a forum with a **giant** market. It had different levels for shopping and for business.

Part of the forum is the *basilica*. It's where important things to do with running the city happen.

There are stalls inside these arches.

How did they pay for things?

Cash only please! Romans used coins made of copper, bronze, silver or gold – gold was the best! Usually the coins had an emperor's face stamped on them, or an emperor's wife.

What about their army?

Funny you should ask! Romans are famous for their gigantic, **highly** trained army. It was so big, it was divided into lots and lots of parts.

How big was this GIGANTIC army?

Thousands of non-citizens were assistant soldiers called **auxilaries**. Citizen soldiers were called **legionaries**. Eight legionaries shared a tent and made up a **contubernium**.

Ten of them made a **century**.

Six centuries made a **cohort**.

Ten cohorts made a **legion** (about 5,000 men).

Eight men in one tent equals STINKY!

There were around **20-30 legions**. The **First Legion** was the most important.

Where did they live?

On the move, they camped in tents. In places they decided to stay, they built **forts** like this one. Forts were like small towns.

UGH, it sounds horrible?

Yep. But you got food, money and somewhere to sleep. After 25 years, legionaries could leave with enough money to buy a farm. When auxiliaries left, they could become Roman citizens, so men from all over the Empire wanted to join up.

The army wasn't just about soldiering. There were doctors, engineers to design roads and build them, and people to do all the different kinds of jobs needed at a camp or fort.

Soldiers on horseback, the **cavalry**, got to live in the stables with their horses. Maybe better than a tent?

If you were a citizen who could read and write, you might become an officer or a **signifer**. Signifers carried a giant decorated pole for their cohort or century, like a mascot. They also looked after their section's accounts **and they got to wear bear fur.**

Were women in the army?

No, but women and children lived in, or nearby, forts and some went along with troops on the move. Mostly they were the families of officers.

So women didn't fight?!

Well, not in the **Roman** army, but, oh yes, in many places women fought against them.

Queen Amanirenas of Kush (modern Sudan) led her armies in a three-year war against the Romans. She was able to stop the Romans invading any further south into Africa.

Queen Boudicca (this red-headed woman) led a rebellion of British tribes and was known as a fearsome warrior.

HAHA, women are a lot scarier than you think, you puny little Romans!

%@$&!*

What were fun times for Romans?

The biggest, most exciting, fun times for Romans were the gigantic public games called *ludi*! They went to watch them at huge arenas in Rome and all around the Empire.

Ludi were held on public holidays, which happened **a lot**, so everyone could watch. There were fights – people and animals – and **more**. Some of the ludi would seem **extremely** and **unnecessarily** violent to us.

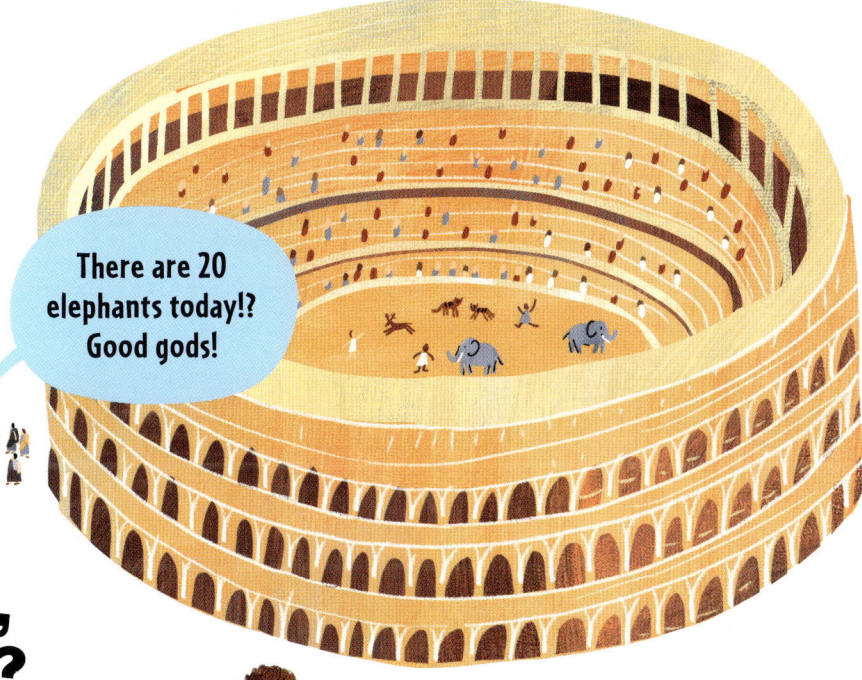

There are 20 elephants today!? Good gods!

What if you wanted QUIET, PEACEFUL fun?

Errrrrr OK then!
There were board games and dice. And children had spinning tops, hobby horses, dolls and many other toys to play with.

Romans loved games that involved betting with money – even though it was against the law. These could become the opposite of **quiet and peaceful**. Children used **nuts** instead of coins.

Get up! You know nothing about the game! Make room for better players!

OK, back to the ludi – which was the most exciting?

It might be chariot racing! Chariot racing was... **innnnsannne**. Chariots pulled by horses raced around a track. Romans **loved** it. They went every Sunday to support their teams.

One of the biggest racetracks was the **Circus Maximus** in Rome. Some say it could fit 250,000 people!

Racers had almost no safety gear.

The chariots are not super sturdy, because they're built to be fast. The **charioteers** need exceptional balance to stay on them.

Only two horses are tied to the chariot. The other two are tied to the driver. If he falls out, the horses will drag him along the track.

I am a REDS fan and I'm doing MAGIC to make them win...

As you can tell, chariot racing was **incredibly** dangerous.

The most thrilling and therefore **awful** crashes were called *naufragia* – which means "shipwreck".

GO BLUES! WE SUPPORT THE BLUES!

I suppose there weren't any cartoons or movies...

Afraid not. Romans had plays instead. There were two kinds – tragedies with sad endings and comedies with happy ones. Comedies probably had more jokes.

All the actors wore masks. This meant you could tell which character was which from **really** far away. There were no women actors – women characters were played by men.

WOWEE – that WAS exciting, what else?

Gladiators! They were trained to fight in packed arenas, **sometimes to the death**. Unfortunately, Romans enjoyed watching gruesome violence in a way we would find **very disturbing**.

There were over 30 different kinds of gladiator. They all had different weapons, costumes and styles of fighting.

I fight with a fishing net and stick with three sharp prongs on it, called a trident.

My style of fighting is like a pretend soldier in a mini battle.

Gladiators were enslaved people, prisoners of war or criminals. They didn't usually have a choice about fighting for other people's entertainment.

Winners could earn fame, money and after a long time... a wooden sword, which meant their **freedom**.

If a gladiator was freed, he could run his own gladiator training school or become a bodyguard to the rich and famous.

CELADUS THE THRAEX IS THE HEART-THROB OF THE GIRLS

Super hands!

People waved their hands to show whether they wanted a defeated gladiator to die or not. But historians aren't sure what signs they made – thumbs up, thumbs down, hiding thumbs!?

Gladiator merch

Romans loved gladiator souvenirs, like these little models. They also painted gladiators in frescoes and on the sides of vases and jugs.

What about all the enslaved people?

Well, while some Romans were having **a whale of a time**, there were hundreds of thousands of enslaved people who had to work for **free**. They worked in the countryside, in cities, in shops and businesses, and in some ordinary homes as well as wealthy ones.

Who were they?

All kinds of people – men, women, young, old... They were from all over the place, captured in war or sold into slavery. Some people sold themselves in desperation, because they were so poor. Others were born enslaved.

What did they do?

All kinds of hard work, mostly.
It could be digging in mines or quarries, or building roads and aqueducts.

Rich people owned hundreds of enslaved people. If they had impressive skills, they were very valuable and expensive to buy. People owned by the emperor might have had a more comfortable life and were even seen as more important than many citizens.

This is sad and scary.

It is. The Romans thought about many things in ways we don't. Slavery is one of them. They didn't question owning people – however fond of them they might be. It was a normal part of the ancient world.

Enslaved people did rebel. They sometimes did this by doing their jobs slowly or accidentally-on-purpose making mistakes.

We know that writers often complained about them being slow. But some also wrote that they shouldn't be punished cruelly.

Were people enslaved forever?

They didn't have to be. Owners could free them if they chose to. Some were allowed to earn money, which meant they could buy their own freedom. These people were known as *freedmen* and *freedwomen*. They could then become citizens themselves.

We know that enslaved people were regularly set free, but we don't know exactly how often.

Sometimes people even escaped.

Did they have a religion?

Well, they had loads of gods and goddesses – one for every single thing you can think of – and all kinds of festivals. People in the Empire were allowed to pray to whoever they liked. But there were three **very important** ones most people followed.

I am Jupiter, the king and MOST IMPORTANT of all gods!

I am Juno, Jupiter's wife... and VERY complicated.

I am the goddess of wisdom, music, law, justice, warfare, a LOT of things.

Jupiter
King of the gods, based on the Greek sky-god and king of the gods *Zeus*. Romans liked Zeus so much, they made him their own. In fact, a few Roman gods and goddesses were copied from Greek ones.

Juno
The goddess of women and childbirth, and the mother of lots of other gods and goddesses.

Minerva
One of Jupiter's daughters. She burst out of his head, as an adult, ready for battle. As you do if you're a goddess.

Who were the rest?

There really were **lots** of gods – and **lots** of stories, or **myths**, about them. You would need a **whole book**, or maybe a **library**, to fit them all in.

"Venus was my name!"

"You can tell who I am because I'm always in the sea with my pointy trident."

Mars
God of war. Soldiers prayed to him to help them win in battle. They called him "Marching Mars," as he marched with them on the battlefield. He was also god of farming.

Venus
The goddess of beauty and lovvvvve. And in the city of Rome, of war, too! Also having a romance with Mars.

Neptune
God of the seas and water – also, randomly, horses!? He wasn't **extremely** important to Romans, unless they were **sailors** or lived by the sea.

Later on in Roman times, an emperor named **Theodosius** made **Christianity** the official religion of the Empire. The dates of some Roman festivals were used for new Christian ones. But some people just stayed with the old gods.

Did they pray?

Yep, prayed and left offerings for the gods – little presents or sometimes big ones. These could be food or drinks or animals they had killed especially! Offerings were for when you wanted some help or if you thought you'd **upset** them – not a good idea.

Shrines were small places to leave offerings.

PLEASE make my hair curl, BIG THANKS!

Romans had shrines at home to pray to household spirits called **lares**. There were also **temples** – big grand buildings where priests and priestesses looked after the gods. At festivals, big ceremonies were held outside.

What were festivals like?

Some were celebrated quietly at home, but others were **huge** street parties. A big one was **Saturnalia** – **eight whole days** in December for **Saturn**, the father of Jupiter and Juno. There was a **mega** party. No one went to work or school, and enslaved people were allowed to do or say **whatever they wanted** for the whole festival. "Io Saturnalia!" was how people said **cheers!**

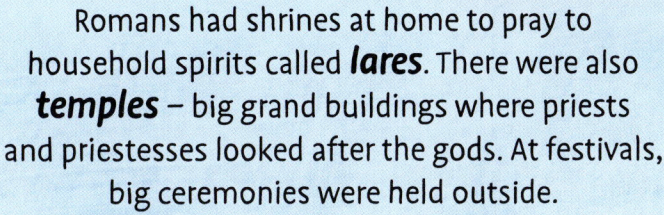

Io Saturnali-nali-nali-aaaa...

BURRRP!

Io Saturnalia!

Important Roman words

Aqueduct – a channel to bring fresh water to towns and cities.

Auxiliary – an ordinary soldier in the army who wasn't a Roman citizen.

Basilica – a building for important business in the forum.

Barbarians – people outside the Empire.

Bathhouse – where people went for a wash and steam, and maybe to exercise.

Cavalry – soldiers on horseback.

Century – about eight tents of soldiers or **centurions**.

Chariot racing – one of the Romans' top fun things to watch, where teams of chariots driven by **charioteers** raced around an arena.

Citizen, Roman – someone with special rights in the Empire.

Codex – the first type of book Romans made.

Cohort – six centuries of soldiers.

Contubernium – eight soldiers stinking up a tent.

Decanus – the leader of a stinky tent (see above).

Domus – a fancy house in the city.

Empire – all the places ruled by an **emperor**.

Enslaved people – people owned by other people, with no rights, and who have to work for free.

Fibula – a brooch to hold clothes together.

Fort – a set of buildings for soldiers to live in.

Forum – a public square for hanging out in Roman towns and cities.

Freedman, freedwoman – a man or woman who used to be enslaved.

Fresco – a funky wall painting.

Gladiator – someone who fought to entertain people, **not by choice**.

Insula – a Roman apartment building.

Lares – household gods.

Latin – the Romans' language.

Legion – ten cohorts, about a thousand **legionaries**.

Ludi – public games, such as gladiator fights and chariot racing.

Ludus – a school for children under eleven (not to be confused with ludi).

Macellum – a food market.

Marble – lovely shiny stone people made into buildings, statues and furniture.

Mosaic – a picture or pattern made of tiny stones, probably on the floor.

Myth – an ancient story about gods and goddesses and magical things.

Naufragia – a really bad crash at a chariot race.

Paedogogus – an enslaved person who took a child to school and looked after them there.

Palla – a woman's cloak.

Papyrus – like paper but made of reeds.

Pessoi – tiny bits of pottery used to scrape your bottom clean.

Pilum – a throwing spear.

Scroll – a rolled-up bit of papyrus or animal skin with writing on.

Senate – important building where important things were decided by important people.

Senator – a very wealthy and important Roman citizen who could vote in the Senate.

Shrine – a place dedicated to a particular god or goddess.

Signifer – the person who carried a cohort or legion's standard, a thing like a banner, in the army.

Stola – a dress.

Strigil – a tool for scraping stinky sweat and dirt off your body.

Stylus – a pen for writing on a wax tablet.

Temple – a big religious building.

Tersorium – a sponge on a stick, maybe for cleaning the toilet or maybe... yourself.

Thermopolium – café with hot food.

Toga – really long piece of fabric only citizens were allowed to wear.

Tonsor – a men's hairdresser or barber.

Tunic – a sort of long top or dress.

Villa – a big country house.

Wax tablet – a board with wax to scratch words on.

Index

Aegyptus, 5
apartments, 13
Apollo, 42
aqueducts, 19
army, 28-32

barbarians, 5
basilica, 27
bathhouses, 16-17, 19
beauty products, 11
beds, 15
bling, 10
books, 23

Ceres, 42
chariot racing, 34-35
Christianity, 41
Circus Maximus, 34

clothes, 8-9, 26

Diana, 42

emperors, 4, 6, 12, 27, 29
    Caligula, 6
    Hadrian, 4, 12
    Theodosius, 41
    Trajan, 27

enslaved people, 7, 12, 15, 36, 38-39
Europe, 4-5

festivals, 43
forts, 28, 31
forums, 27
freedmen, freedwomen, 39
frescoes, 14, 15
fun, 33-37

games, 33-37
gladiators, 36-37
gods and goddesses, 40-43

Hadrian's Wall, 4
hair, 10-11
homes, 12-15

Italy, 3

Julius Caesar, 4
Juno, 40
Jupiter, 40

kitchens, 15

Latin, 4, 5, 23
lights, 14

Mare Nostrum, 5
markets, 24-25, 27
Mars, 41
Mercury, 42
Minerva, 40
money, 27
mosaics, 15
myths, 41

Neptune, 41
North Africa, 4-5

plays, 35
prayers, 43

queens, 32
    Amanirenas of Kush, 32
    Boudicca, 32

religion, 40-43
Roman citizens, 7, 28, 31, 39
Roman Empire, 3, 4-5
Rome, 3, 5
Romulus and Remus, 4

Saturnalia, 43
schools, 20-23
Senate, the, 6

senators, 6
sewers, 19
shopping, 24-27
shops, 13, 24-27
slavery, 38-39
soldiers, 28-32

temples, 43
toilets, 13, 18, 19

Venus, 41
Vesta, 42
villas, 12
Vulcan, 42

water, 19
West Asia, 4-5
wigs, 11
writing, 21

47